Amazon FBA Expert

An Expert Guide to Master Amazon FBA.

CONNECTION

BOOKS CLUB

TABLE OF CONTENTS

Introduction

In this book, we address the many problems and concerns readers of our first book *Fulfillment by Amazon: Step-by-step Instructions to Start a Fulfillment by Amazon Business* faced in their beginning stages as both an Amazon vendor and a Fulfillment by Amazon (FBA) vendor. This book identifies their problems and concerns, and presents researched advice from Amazon published sources and vendors' feedbacks collated over several years, and from as many discussion forums as was plausible. This book also considers some of the updated regulations by Amazon in 2017, and gives expert advice on managing these changes. These changes could affect a vendor's decision on how to plan for sales and stock for the short and the long term. In short, this expert book is a one-stop book for Amazon vendors to leverage on the benefits of FBA, and to procure suggestions from other experts on how they manage their businesses on the platform.

Let us reiterate the basic guiding principle on how to benefit by using FBA: to focus on selling. We shall examine the methods available to maximize profits by managing cost price and selling prices; give ideas on how to overtake your competitors to direct sales to your shop rather than theirs; and give tips on which virtual tools and services available in the Amazon ecosystem which Amazon vendors can use to carve out their competitive edge.

Receive Your Special Gift

Thank you for your purchase of this eBook! I hope you enjoy reading this eBook as much as I enjoyed writing it. As part of your purchase, I invite you to join my email subscribers. This FREE subscription lets you receive a newsletter, highlighting the great new books available from Connection Books Club and other exclusive business and self-development information. Subscribing is easy, and members receive great deals and fantastic eBooks at a discount! All you need to do is click this link to enter your email:

http://www.connectionbooksclub.com/bonus/

In addition to this great opportunity to subscribe to incredible discounts and our newsletter, as a welcome gift, you'll receive a FREE eBook download! Learn how to secure your financial future with the informative eBook, *Money Management: Learn How to Organize Your Financial Life and Invest in Your Future.* It's yours for FREE once you've enrolled! http://www.connectionbooksclub.com/bonus/

Welcome to the club, and we hope you enjoy your purchase as well as our FREE welcome gift! Click the picture below

Have you ever wished that you were better with money?

Do you ever find yourself being overwhelmed by the state of your personal finances?

Would you like to become more financially responsible?

Now you can, with **5 Reasons to Invest in Money Management: Learn How to Organize Your Financial Life and Invest in Your Future**, a short self-help book that is packed with information on how to make the most of your financial situation.

If you want to be able to lower your interest rates, learn up to date money management strategies and turn your financial situation into one of prosperity and stability, then you'll find the answers inside, with solid advice that includes:

➢ Strategies which are designed for the average person
➢ Your options for retirement
➢ Hacks for navigating the grocery store's subtle spending traps
➢ Ways to pay less than you owe on credit cards and other outstanding debts
➢ Finding freedom with financial stability

Suitable for complete novices, **5 Reasons to Invest in Money Management** is a book that will transform the way you look at and deal with your finances.

Download a free copy and start investing in your future today!

http://www.connectionbooksclub.com/bonus/

Prosperity is waiting for **YOU!**

1. Foundations of FBA

1.1 Consider a Professional seller plan

A vendor may choose to remain on an Individual seller plan or change to go on a Professional seller plan. Both seller plans can engage the Fulfillment by Amazon (FBA) service. Orders that do not use FBA, or the Amazon fulfillment network (AFN) goods of which are stored and processed in Amazon fulfillment centers, are generally termed as merchant-fulfilled orders.

The common calculation to indicate when this change makes business sense is if a vendor can sell more than 40 units in a month. The number of units is derived by dividing the monthly fee of using FBA by the per order service fee charged for Individual seller accounts. It thus is also usually deemed as a less profitable combination of fees when a vendor includes a FBA monthly fee on top of its per order service fee. This is a plausible reason however if there is a large enough profit margin on the goods, and if the vendor is trying to get a larger geographical reach of customers.

The purpose of this book is to focus on generating sales. Its aim is to sell more than 40 units a month, and thus the suggestion to consider using a Professional seller plan.

1.2 Understand your seller account settings

(Objective of this section is to familiarize the new settings that will show up on a Professional seller's account who is using FBA. I need to get access to such an account to list the new tools available for the Professional seller to utilize.)

EXPERT TIP: Before you change the email address of your account, note that Amazon will send an email to the email address that is currently registered in your seller's account to verify the authenticity of this new action. Be sure you can still log in to the currently registered email address to retrieve Amazon's message to successfully complete this change of email address action.

1.3 Insuring Your Professional Seller Account

This is an often neglected aspect of a professional seller. A professional seller account on Amazon comes with its perks and are accordingly required to have the tools that protect professional businesses. Vendors will professional selling plans are required to provide proof of Commercial General Liability insurance is able to cover up to $1,000,000 per occurrence, and must include products liability, bodily injury, personal injury, and property damage amongst other protections. The insurance can either be in a single policy or a combination of policies so long as they satisfy the limits as stipulated by Amazon. Vendors are required to be in an original document, and have to be sent via mail or email.

EXPERT TIP: Ensure that the following wordings "Amazon.com, Inc. its affiliates and assignees are additional insureds, as their interests may appear" are in your policy. Vendors can find more information about the required insurance requirements in their Participation Agreements.

EXPERT TIP: There are account suspension insurances available that help suspended account holders appeal to Amazon. They guarantee success within a short time period so that selling can continue, or then offer to make a pay out to the vendor.

Enjoying your eBook so far? Take a moment to subscribe to our FREE newsletter for incredible discounts, books giveaways, and VIP offers!

> ➤ http://www.connectionbooksclub.com/bonus/

All we need is your email, and you'll be set up to receive more of the eBooks you can't wait to read.

2. What to sell when leveraging on Fulfillment by Amazon

The objective of this section is to align a vendor to the customer-loyalty strategies of Amazon. By studying how Amazon attracts and retains their customers, vendors who can supply products and services to piggyback on Amazon's initiatives will probably find better return on investment when utilizing the services Amazon has designed for its vendors to match these initiatives.

The main benefit of subscribing to a Fulfillment by Amazon (FBA) is that the customers benefit that most, and thus return to keep buying from Amazon. It is perhaps interesting at this point to see from a customer's perspective why when vendors use FBA, it pleases the customers better:

- Amazon customers enjoy FREE SHIPPING.
- Amazon Prime customers enjoy not only free shipping, but also a quick two-day delivery of their orders.
- Amazon customers are able to sift out the most competitive prices of the products they wish to purchase without buffered in or inflated costs of shipping or packaging.
- Amazon customers trust in the Fulfillment by Amazon logo, and rather than dealing with possible varying standards of Individual merchants, tend to trust that Amazon will handle the packing, delivery, customer service, and returns to their best interests.
- Amazon customers like to enjoy the convenience of gift-wrapping services and up-to-the-minute countdown for one-day shipping orders.

To encourage vendors from continue to provide a good range of products to their customers, FBA offers the benefits of managing for a vendor the entire process from processing orders to collecting reviews with the FBA service. What is more interesting, and which is the basis of maximizing sales when using FBA, is the ability for vendors to access data on Amazon customer behaviors, and to fulfill orders from other non-Amazon sales channels.

2.1 Make your product relevant to Amazon subscription members

The Amazon customers who enjoy the shopping privileges detailed in the previous chapter usually have an Amazon membership in the form of a subscription. At the point of writing, Amazon has five membership programs: Prime Student, Amazon @ Your University, Amazon Family (previously Amazon Mom), Amazon Prime, and AmazonSmile. Amazon membership subscribers are loyal to the program they have subscribed to, and are cost-savvy to opt for vendors who will offer free shipping amongst the other benefits from their program.

EXPERT TIP: By sourcing for products relevant to these subscription members, and continuing to support Amazon's priority to offer its members their continued benefits of savings, convenience, and great customer experience, a vendor can tap into a ready base of repeating, trusting customers with even more support from Amazon.

Amazon Prime

The implied number of Amazon Prime members is suggested to be approximately 65 million at the beginning of 2017. Data also suggests that Amazon Prime members spend 4.6 times more than non-Prime members, and about 40 per cent of Prime members spend more than $1,000 a year compared to just 8 per cent of non-Prime members.

Here is a snapshot of what Amazon Prime members get for a $99 annual fee: free two-day shipping, free same-day shipping for eligible zip codes, free two-hour delivery for Prime Now items in eligible zip codes, free restaurant delivery within Prime Now zip codes, free release-date delivery on eligible pre-order items, unlimited video streaming of movies and TV episodes on Prime Video, unlimited ad-free music from on Prime Music, secured unlimited photo storage in Prime Photos, access to Prime Pantry for a flat delivery fee of $5.99 (which is waivered on some conditions), access to Amazon Elements products, access to Amazon Dash for Prime with Amazon Dash Button, Prime Early Access for lighting deals, access to Kindle Owner's Lending Library, access to Prime Reading, free download of a new book per month on Kindle First, add-on subscriptions to Amazon Music Unlimited and Video add-on subscriptions, access to deals and discounts from Amazon Family, exclusive discounts on Twitch Prime, and Membership Sharing.

When vendors remove shipping costs concerns from their products by using Fulfillment by Amazon (FBA) and make their products eligible for Prime customers' benefits, they can focus on sales strategies for to source relevant products for Amazon Prime customers.

EXPERT TIP: By keeping up-to-date with the popular membership plans, vendors can source smartly the products that are following Amazon customer focus and trends.

Prime Student

Prime Student or Amazon Student is a program designed to market Amazon services to the 21 million college students in the US with a spending power of $545 billion a year. Statistics show that 44 per cent of fulltime college students visit Amazon at least once a month and a Prime Student purchases two and a half times more on Amazon than an average Amazon buyer. The program uses social media, on-site promotions, emails, and a brand ambassador program that offers peer-to-peer interaction with your brand and products. Prime Student offers a six-month trial period and a 50 per cent off subscription fee on Amazon Prime to enjoy the same privileges as an Amazon Prime subscriber. Prime Students need to be above 18 years old and have a valid .edu email account to qualify.

EXPERT TIP: Source products that are relevant to a Prime Student. Recall what matters to a student whether they are living at home or in dormitories. School supplies, stationery, dorm decorations, dorm essentials, trendy and creative attire accessories, electronics, hobby and sports equipment, sentimental gifts and messages of support for examination or stressful periods, popular leisure reading books and magazines, and craft supplies are products that can cater to the Prime Student demographic.

Baby Registry @ Amazon

Amazon provides a service to expectant parents to open an online registry account on Amazon where they can add to their wish list both Amazon items and non-Amazon online times. The service is very attractive because of the convenient manner registrants can add items to their wish list, track which gifts loved ones have purchased for them, organize thank-you messages, manage returns for items they have second thoughts about, and a 15 per cent discount off the purchased value of their wish list that they can use to purchase additional items on Amazon 60 days before their baby is due.

EXPERT TIP: Source products that expectant parents would find useful and beautiful for their babies and their room. If you have in storage seasonal products for babies' prams and weather protection, this is a good way to attach it with a coupon or incentive, so that parents can preplan the needs of their babies and be grateful to buy in advance good deals for off-season products, since they can utilize their discount money wisely. Other useful looking-ahead products include childproofing items, extra bedding, and sensory toys for babies. When you have a suitable product for a baby's elder brother or big sister, list and describe them as potential gift ideas. This can attract expectant parents to use their discount money to get a present for the baby's siblings, something that most parents do practice to help manage potential feelings of jealousy, but that are not appropriate to add to a baby registry wish list.

Prime Family

Prime Family, Amazon Family, or Amazon Mom, is a free membership that all Amazon Prime members can enjoy. Customers only require a child's birth date to qualify for a Prime Family account.

EXPERT TIP: Prime Family members receive standard discounts for diapers, but also regular discounts from Subscribe and Save. Consider different family needs when sourcing products for sale. Families with a larger number of young children will benefit from this service, and so will families who have elderly and handicapped members. Study diet trends, observe which items are bulky and heavy, and which items shoppers tend to wish to have privacy about at the checkout line as these are the items that shoppers will be happy to utilize free shipping to have shipped conveniently and discreetly to their homes. Whilst shoppers do enjoy visiting the grocery shop, there are items that give less shopping pleasure than others, and these are the attractive items to have shipped in the neat Amazon Prime box.

STEM Club

Stem Club is a subscription service unveiled in January 2017 that delivers STEM toys to subscribers monthly, for a monthly fee of $19.99. STEM toys are toys designed for children to engage actively with educational toys relating to the subjects of Science, Technology, Engineering, and Mathematics. The toys are handpicked by Amazon, and categorized into suitability for age groups three to four, five to seven, and eight to thirteen years old.

Subscribe and Save

Subscribe and Save is a subscription service that aims to alleviate an Amazon Prime member's stress of running out of essential household goods, by offering them the convenience of frequently replenishing the products to their homes, on a predetermined and easily amended date and frequency. It is a very popular subscription program for its convenience, and the extra savings subscribers may enjoy by listing five or more subscription-eligible products for a same day delivery.

This used to be an Amazon product only platform, and is now offered to Fulfillment by Amazon vendors.

Prime Pantry

Prime Pantry allows Prime subscribers to buy regular grocery items in small quantities, almost like a weekly shopping list. It has a delivery fee of $5.99 and a regular delivery time of four days. If members select five items from the Prime Pantry list of items, the delivery fee is waivered.

EXPERT TIP: A vendor would have to pack these items in small or even single quantities to fit the marketing initiative of this program. The items in Prime Pantry tend to be consumed quickly and need to be replenished frequently. However, they have to withstand a logistic turnaround time of four to five days, and thus is an unsuitable sales initiative for highly-perishable goods.

2.2 Work market segments

If a vendor feels unable or unwilling to tackle the Amazon place with products deliberately designed or sourced to cater to the Amazon customer-loyalty programs, there is another way to identify what products are suitable to sell by FBA, and what sales strategies to consider therefore.

There are two market segments that goods sold on Amazon fall under: high-involvement purchase goods and low-involvement purchase goods.

High-Involvement Purchase Goods

High-involvement purchase goods are either goods that are more expensive and require longer decision-making time; or goods that give high emotional satisfaction when successfully procured, and as well disappointment when the product feel short of their expectations.

Items that are considered high-involvement purchase goods are products that

- cater to personal tastes, e.g. clothing, shoes, beauty products, health and personal care products, groceries and gourmet food, pet supplies

10

- cater to personal lifestyle, e.g. computers and accessories, electronics, sports and outdoor equipment
- are related to the home and are shared by members of the family, e.g. home and kitchen appliances, home improvement products, dining ware.

Customers who use Amazon for high-involvement purchase goods require lots of reassurance in the form of reviews, extra information, and detailed product images as part of their research on the product before buying-in.

Low-Involvement Purchase Goods

Low-involvement purchase goods on the other hand are purchases that are lower in costs, and in emotional attachment.

Customers who use Amazon for these purchases generally do not leave many reviews and the categories include office products, toys and games, costume jewelry, musical instruments, arts and crafts, sewing materials, industrial and scientific equipment, watches, and patio, lawn, and garden products.

Determining which market segments you would like to source products for to sell will affect the methods you will use to attract buyers.

2.3 Follow the trends

At the point of writing this book, the most popular items to sell on Amazon include paleo bars, bow ties, pocket squares, wooden sunglasses, wooden watches, leggings, e-cigarettes, coconut oil, and matcha powder.

There is no saying what is next month's trends or next season's trends, but when Amazon buyers follow trends, the general pattern for sales is fast moving growth for a few months and then the sales will slow down. Be careful not to be stuck with large stockpiles and storage costs for over-ordering trend items, as trends generally do not revive in the short term.

EXPERT TIP: A way to ride the trends waves is to pay close attention to the topics discussed in social media, and to study fashion and diet tips on monthly fashion and lifestyle magazines.

EXPERT TIP: Take note of Meltable FBA Inventory requirements if you decide to follow a food trend. They are only accepted at certain months of the year, require an expiration date, must be able to be stored between 50 to 100 degrees F, and if stored in glasses must be less than 4 ounces in volume, and survive various drop tests and vigorous shaking tests.

EXPERT TIP: A ranking of a product can be displayed by the category it is in, and the sub-category that it is correlated with. It is a fluctuating number that is affected by the hourly demand and supply for the product in relation to other products within the same category. Be sure to assess the performance of the product by the main category that it is in to get the accurate information on its product performance.

2.4 Products prohibited on Amazon FBA

When a vendor considers using FBA, it is important to consider the further criteria required by Amazon FBA that may not apply to a merchant-fulfilled product:

- The product has to be allowed to be lawfully sold in ALL US jurisdictions;
- The product has to weigh less than 150 pounds, and is less than 144 inches by 96 inches by 96 inches in size;
- The product is not a safety hazard to the FBA warehouse facilities;
- The product has to be prepared strictly according to FBA stipulations to allow a smooth workflow from product identification to delivery; and
- The product cannot be defective or damaged.

EXPERT TIP: Some items specifically mentioned are alcoholic beverages, counterfeit products, vehicle tires, gift cards, and loose packaged batteries. Some other items that are prohibited for sale on Amazon include Native American artifacts, Kinder surprise eggs, Oscar statuettes, lawn darts, cribs made before 28 June 2011, products containing feathers of migratory birds, products containing nicotine, prescription lenses, lottery tickets, fuel, pets, real estate, and cars. These products should not be confused with restricted products that require an extra approval, or a vetting, process from Amazon.

When identifying if your product is eligible for FBA, first check if they are legally allowed on Amazon, then if they match the FBA allowed criteria, if you can prepare your product according to the stipulations of FBA, and if you can readily decide how to dispose of or have damaged or defective goods sent back to you. If you cannot make all of these criteria, the goods can be disposed without reimbursement, and a record will be made against your vendor performance towards Amazon.

Enjoying your eBook so far? Take a moment to subscribe to our FREE newsletter for incredible discounts, books giveaways, and VIP offers!

> ➢ http://www.connectionbooksclub.com/bonus/

All we need is your email, and you'll be set up to receive more of the eBooks you can't wait to read.

3. How to manage Amazon's expectations of inventory quality control when using FBA

Fulfillment by Amazon consists of five steps: 1) A vendor sends the product to Amazon. 2) Amazon stores the products. 3) A customer orders your product. 4) Amazon picks and packs your products. 5) Amazon ships your products.

Vendors only have to work on steps one and three of the entire process: sending the products to Amazon, and creating sales for the products.

Amazon is serious about providing satisfaction consumer experiences for the buyer, and thus has a large list of stipulations vendors can work with to jointly fulfill this objective. This section will provide expert tips on how to send a product to Amazon. It is the most important step, as failure to do so will trip the entire process for your sales if this vital step is not done to the fullest satisfaction of Amazon that it requires for enabling the best customer experience. Until your product reaches step three, everything in step one will ensure your product stays in step two of the process.

3.1 How to send a product to Amazon Fulfillment Centers

Here are some fast tips that will help you glide through the FBA requirements.

1. Ensure that your product has an eligible barcode.

The FBA facility runs with barcodes. Both manufacturer and Amazon barcodes are eligible barcodes. Barcodes have to be scan-able for 24 months from the date it arrives at the facility.

If you use a manufacturer's barcode, your product will be comingled with that of other sellers who are using the same barcode number to sell the same product. The manufacturer's barcode has to be visible on the product for examination without Amazon having to remove any prep packaging.

Amazon barcodes, ASIN and FNSKU, are used for products that do not already have manufacturer barcodes, but also include products that require control if they have expiration dates. If a product requires an ASIN, it has to be pasted over the manufacturer barcode so that Amazon will track it only by its ASIN.

2. Ensure that your product accurately matches the condition it is stated as. This includes your external packaging, i.e. how the package (that is intended to be shipped to customers) arrives at Amazon.

Products listed as New need to be in pristine condition, that have never been unpacked. A slight dent on the packaging box will need to have appropriate comments that state the imperfect part of the item.

EXPERT TIP: Your products are examined when they arrive at the Amazon fulfillment facility. If your product has been listed as 'New' but shows signs of wear, they are not relabeled as 'Used', but rather are listed as 'Unsellable'. Vendors are advised to ensure their carriers are responsible for the condition the goods arrive in.

3. Ensure that your product is correctly prepped and ready for fulfillment.

Different types of products require different attention to packaging. The purpose of these specific packaging requires are not for esthetic reasons, but are to ensure that minimum time is wasted for received inventory to be scanned, stored, retrieved, packed, and shipped to the customer. Ensure that your prep is according to its specifications, or the your products will be reassigned to the problem solvers and the delay can take up to two days, with possible extra costs and remarks to your account.

For products that contain liquids:

- The volume for liquids in glass containers have to be less than four ounces, and liquids in non-glass containers have to be less than five gallons (or 20 lbs).
- The product has to be of a standard size and not exceed: 1) 20 pounds in weight, and 2) 18 inches (longest side), 14 inches (median side), and 8 inches (shortest side).
- The containers require a double seal. A double seal consists of: 1) a tightened lid, and 2) a manufacturer's seal, often either as safety peel-off seal or a seal around the rim of the container. If the container does not have the second seal, it can be prepped by the vendor with polybags or shrinkwrap. Ensure that the plastic prep materials are printed with suffocation warning labels. If the bag is not self-adhesive, use tape to seal the bag so that the item does not separate from the bag.
- The barcode of the product must be easily scan-able without needed to open the package or the prep materials.
- The prepped product must survive without leakage or breakage, a five-stepped, three-foot drop test. At a height of three-feet, drop the prepped item five times sequentially on a hard floor, first on its bottom, then its top, then its longest side, then its shortest side, and finally on its edge.

EXPERT TIP: Use polybags that are at least 1.5m, and add a clearly visible suffocation warning for bags that are large than 5 inches.

For products that contain pellets, powders, or garnula:

- Products that contain loose pellets, powders, or granula require prepping in polybags to ensure the contents do not come loose while in transport or in storage. This includes compact powders, that when dropped break into powder pieces.

For products that are breakable and fragile:

- Products that are fragile or breakable should be bubble wrapped or have an overwrap box. The products should be wrapped individually even if they are sold in a pack or a set. Products with multiple sides, e.g. six-sided, should be wrapped so that each side is protected.
- The prepped products should withstand the drop test and an additional four-minute vigorous shaking test.

The label should be easily scan-able without having to remove the prepping of the product.

EXPERT TIP: For items that are Plexiglas, stick a 2 x 3-inch label on the packaging clearly stating that this is Plexiglas. Otherwise, it may be considered as a glass item that requires fragile prepping.

For products that contain lithium batteries:

- Lithium or products that include lithium batteries need to have rigid packaging. This includes being packed in the manufacturer's packaging, boxes, or clamshell plastic containers. Regular shrinkwrap or plastic bags are not considered rigid packaging.
- The products have to be tested for a five-step four-foot drop. The steps are similar to that of glass prepping, but lithium batteries require a four-foot rather than the usual three-foot drop height.

EXPERT TIP: Products containing lithium when not transported or stored carefully can react hazardously to heat. Aim to sell manufacturer-packaged lithium products, and if selling toys that require batteries, a vendor can opt to state clearly that batteries are not included in the product offering.

For products made from woven materials: This category includes apparels, fabrics, textiles, and plush toys, and care is taken that the quality of the product is not compromised by dust, humidity, or tearing. The criteria is an exposure of one inch by one inch to qualify the product for special packaging.

- The product has to be wrapped in a transparent polybag with a suffocation warning or shrinkwrapped so that the surface of the product is protected throughout the fulfillment process. Ensure that the packaging does not protrude more than three inches past the dimensions of the product. When possible, use a cardboard backing for the product before prepping. Wrap shoes in a pair in a bag.
- Ensure that the barcode or ASIN sticker of the product is easily scan-able without removing the packaging of the product.

EXPERT TIP: For textiles that can be damaged from plastic wrapping, prep them in a box and then prep the box with plastic wrap. Shoeboxes of collector's shoes items should be prepped them carefully with bubble wrap so that the box is not damaged.

For product with sharp edges:

- Wrap the product in plastic wrap, or a blister pack to ensure that the sharp edge will not be exposed throughout the fulfillment process. Ensure that the sharp edge cannot cut through the packaging.
- Use dunnage when necessary to ensure the packages do not move during transportation.
- Ensure that the label is scan-able without having to remove the prepping.

For jewelry:

- Jewelry sold in pouches or boxes require prepping for the fulfillment process to ensure they do not get damaged and dusty. A fitting transparent polybag with a suffocation warning, or a box sleeve is suitable for prepping. Ensure that the prep materials allow the product to fit snugly so that they do not come loose during fulfillment, or damaged.
- Ensure that the barcode with a product description is easily scan-able without Amazon having to remove the sleeve or the polybag.

EXPERT TIP: The default replacement value of jewelry is $50. If your high-value jewelry items exceed the $2,000 replacement value, note that you might need to provide additional receipts to prove the item's value. Amazon will take into consideration several factors prior to assessing a replacement value, and only if they are not able to find a replacement item, that includes the average selling price for the item on Amazon. Thus, ensure that your jewelry items follow the guidelines for sale stipulated, and are prepped perfectly to standards. If an item is valued higher than $5,000, it is advised for the vendor to take up third-party insurance.

For adult products:

- Adult products must be packed in black, opaque bags with suffocation warnings.
- The ASIN barcode must be clearly scan-able on the bag.

EXPERT TIP: There are acceptable suggestive texts allowed, but obscenity, profanity, and images of models in suggestive positions are not acceptable for fulfillment. It is best to check with Amazon directly prior to sending the shipment.

For food and beverage products:

Apart from using the specific prep materials to suit the product's packaging, e.g. for items that are breakable or that require a double seal, food and beverage items are required to be clearly labeled when they are date and temperature sensitive. Ensure that your expiration date labels are specified as follows:

- The date formats to list expiration dates are either MM-YYYY or MM-DD-YYYY.
- The label must cover up any manufactured date information. This means that no other date must be visible to Amazon associates except for the expiration dates.
- The label must be printed with a 36-point font or larger.
- There must be labels for both the master carton, i.e. the shipment package, and on each individual product unit.
- Products need to have a shelf life of last 105 days when Amazon receives, and is disposed of by Amazon when it has less than 50 days shelf life. These goods are considered expired, and will not be eligible for returns.
- Consider how the product is consumed when calculating an expiry date. A daily supplement of a hundred pills will require a shelf life of a hundred days or more. Add in a

shelf life buffer as any product that has less than 50 days shelf life will be disposed off by Amazon.

- Products that have different expiration dates cannot be packed in the same shipment box as each SKU can only contain a type of date-expiration content. Note that the vendor would have to pack them in separate shipment boxes with different box contents labels.
- Products that are subject to melting will only be accepted by Amazon between October, 1 and April 30, of the calendar year, and when not assigned to be returned, will be disposed off by May, 1.

EXPERT TIP: Note that products that have expiration labels cannot be commingled, and when unsold, will incur either a per product unit disposal fee or a per product unit return fee.

EXPERT TIP: It is very important not to use shredded paper, small loose pieces (including foam peanuts and foam strips), and crinkle wrap as dunnage. Use bubble wrap, inflatable air pillows, full sheets of heavy weight kraft paper, or polyethylene foam sheeting.

EXPERT TIP: Opt for case packed items for shipment to Amazon fulfillment centers if you have multiple quantities of the same product, in identical condition, and have the same SKU. Enter the quantity of units per case, and how many identical cases accurately when filling out the shipment plan, and be sure that the information is exactly how the supplier or manufacturer will be packing the products they are sending before giving this information to Amazon. Case packed items have to be sent to Amazon in the original manufacturer's box that has printed on it, the quantity of items in the box. Each box requires a SKU label, and the individual items in the box do not need to be individually labeled. Shipping care packed items usually saves shipping costs, as they are sent to one and not more Amazon warehouses, and do not get charged an individual inventory placement fee.

4. Create your shipping plan.

Upon identifying your products for sale, listing them in your inventory, and prepping them according to the stipulations of FBA, a vendor can create a shipping plan to send the products to the Amazon fulfillment centers. Ensure that the shipping label is printed out and clearly labeled onto your shipment that is sent to Amazon. Ensure also that your shipments are sent to the correct fulfillment centre allocated to you, and that the products in your shipment match your shipping plan.

It is also very important to include box content information. This box content information is part of your shipment creation plan. There are four methods to organize your content information on the form. If a vendors intend to ship more than 10 boxes, note that it will take a maximum of 25 SKUs.

EXPERT TIP: If the number of boxes or SKUs exceed that, use either the excel or text template provided to add a packing list, or enable your account to use 2D barcodes to identify the products. These 2D barcodes have to be labeled on the master carton box on the same surface side of the shipping label.

5. Send your shipment to the designated Amazon fulfillment center.

Determine which category your packed products will fall under, in order to select the appropriate shipping method to Amazon fulfillment centers. If possible, consider using Amazon's preferred partner, UPS, to send small parcel deliveries (SPD) to Amazon fulfillment centers, as it is possible that their prices would be more reasonable than other logsitics competitors. There are three reasons for a vendor to make the accurate delivery selection:

- It affects what type of carrier service a vendor should use (some of whom require the vendor to book an appointment using a FBA booking form).
- It affects the shipment calculation cost towards each product sent to the fulfillment center.
- It determines what shipment labels are required.

EXPERT TIP:

3.2 How to avoid being a Problem Unit

All products units that arrive to the fulfillment warehouses are processed by Amazon associates, and those packages that do not meet with any of the many criteria that allows Amazon to smoothly and accurately process a product will be sent to the Amazon warehouse problem solver. The problem solver solves the problems when possible and assigns a prep service fee required per problem unit, or disposes of the product as Unsellable. Here is a quick checklist to help ensure that your shipment to Amazon will be processed smoothly, and be quickly listed for sale.

EXPERT TIP: Amazon identifies the vendors who are not following prep specifications. The fees for a subsequent occurrence for the same problem are almost doubled.

√ Does each product unit have its own barcode?
√ Does each product unit need a label?
√ Does each product unit need poly bagging?
√ Do the poly bags have visible suffocation warning labels?
√ Does each product unit require bubble wrapping?
√ Does each product unit require opaque poly bagging (especially for adult products)?
√ Are the products securely taped to their prep materials so that they do not come loose?

Enjoying your eBook so far? Take a moment to subscribe to our FREE newsletter for incredible discounts, books giveaways, and VIP offers!

➤ http://www.connectionbooksclub.com/bonus/

All we need is your email, and you'll be set up to receive more of the eBooks you can't wait to read.

4. Doing Business on Amazon using FBA

The considerations of sales trends, restrictions and prohibitions, and FBA prepping and shipping criteria might now have some influence on what a vendor feels can and cannot be managed in the short term to sell on Amazon using FBA. It will also begin to create a separate group of ideas for what items can be prepared for longer term sales plans.

Most items will fall under one of the two categories: an arbitrage product, and a private label product. An arbitrage product is an item that is a mere resale item. The item is bought at a lower than usual cost price, and sold at the Amazon average retail price, and the difference, i.e. the profit, is larger than the costs of prepping, costs of shipping to fulfillment centers, and the FBA monthly fees. Vendors source for arbitrage items from a variety of thrift stores, factories, or manufacturers who sell their products online.

EXPERT TIP: Ensure that you have factored in storage costs for inventory products, an allowance for returns that require new prepping, costs for returns for disposal items, and festive season storage surcharges, to have an accurate calculation of what the profits are.

A private label product has the similar business sense of an arbitrage product, but it includes an element of marketing. This is particularly interesting for vendors who are interested to create a story, a brand, a value-add, and a relationship with the customers for a product.

To conduct a successful business on Amazon, a vendor

- Requires a product or a product range, and a target audience in mind.
- Has considered the restrictions on Amazon for this product, and have decided how to manage these restrictions and expectations.
- Has considered and can manage the prepping requirements of Amazon.
- Has a plan on when to enter the selling cycle of Amazon.
- Has a steady supply of products available for sale.

4.1 Procuring Products

Procuring products for most Amazon vendors requires working with other sellers to carve out a margin for themselves. These other sellers could be one or a few of the following types of sellers.

- Manufacturers who invest in the research and development of a product and sell them to vendors.
- Manufacturers who are selling directly to the end user via e-commerce platforms.
- Resellers who are representing manufacturers who do not have an online presence.
- Resellers who are trying to make an arbitrage business between manufacturers and vendors.
- Amazon vendors who are selling the same product, and carving out their best profit margins.

Some platforms that vendors use to source products include Alibaba, Keepa, The Tracktor, CamelCamelCamel, Google, Shopify, 888Lots, Inventory Source, and Esources. Some vendors also liaise with manufacturers in their vicinity, and others contact manufacturers directly from their websites.

EXPERT TIP: Streamline your search to suppliers who are ranked in a higher tier of reliability. For example, when using Alibaba's platform, tick on the Assessed Supplier and Gold Supplier boxes to limit the range of suppliers you would like to deal with. It may not be supplier with the lowest price offering, but these suppliers have successful business experiences.

EXPERT TIP: Install Chrome Browser extensions that can add valuable online tools for product procurements, especially in identifying high-performance products, low-costs sourcing deals, and useful product comparison metrics.

EXPERT TIP: Veteran Amazon FBA vendors prepare their stock for Quarter 4 sales as early as in Spring, to secure products, ensure timely prep and shipping procedures, and launch promotions and creative listings to begin in late Autumn. Inventory is an important criteria for FBA purchases, and securing that space without incurring extra storage costs is a great balance of resources. Some manufacturers who have long-term relationships with good vendors will agree to keep the goods, or part of it, for a short time span at not extra costs so that sellers can save on storage costs in fulfillment centers, in preparation for Q4.

4.2 Buying Wholesale

Buying wholesale is a great way to gain good margins on a product by buying large quantities at low prices. A commonly used wholesale website by Amazon sellers is Alibaba.com. There are however more than 50 great wholesale websites that can be found easily online.

Online wholesale store fronts exist in two main types: The first at the factory itself that manages their online site from their in-house sales teams; the other is a middleman storefront who buys from these wholesale stores and then resells them to buyers.

There are good reasons why middlemen storefronts have their value. Most commonly, they serve to bridge the language and cultural barrier that may exist between Amazon sellers, and manufacturers based in China or who are not proficient in English. They can add value by buying in bulk, and reselling in smaller quantities that is more manageable for Amazon sellers who need to test a product with an introductory order. At times, they perform all the shipping logistics, and the goods are available in the US as opposed to a seller having to manage shipments and related paperwork. Additionally, they usually have all the marketing materials like product images, product descriptions, and perhaps successful selling experience with the product on other e-commerce sites either via their own private label or with other Amazon sellers. With these added value, an Amazon seller who uses a middleman might face a higher price per unit than when going to the manufacturer directly. It is however worth considering that these middlemen are familiar with prices and rankings on Amazon, and know that sellers can still edge out a margin, and now a more comfortable margin, with their services. Avoid those middlemen who provide no added value or service from the processing to feedback stage.

Wholesale products are excellent in providing a lower cost per unit. This is an especially financially-profitable possibility when a wholesale product is then bundled with another wholesale product, that helps create a premium margin over two already high-margin goods. A bundle comes with your own listing page, the high possibility to own your buy box, and great value to the Amazon buyer. Conduct your research by looking out for great wholesale buys from overseas and in the US, and see which categories of products are available readily at wholesale prices. Check these products against Amazon listings to see what products are usually bought together with your main interested product. From there, it is viable to observe the pattern of Amazon buyer behavior to create winning bundles at wholesale prices that can be transferred to the Amazon buyer at a lower price and higher convenience.

For Amazon vendors who are unfamiliar with wholesale, take note that wholesalers are interested to sell to as many people as possible. Their interests comes from a higher return on investment with a larger quantity that they sell. They seldom are exclusive to a vendor, and will give better prices to larger orders. Be sure not to be pressured in bulk buying before proper market research has been conducted, and the product is shown to be well-received and selling well.

EXPERT TIP: Pet products are a good category that sell well on Amazon and are readily available for wholesale buys. Pet products range from beds, blankets, collars, tags (to engrave a name and telephone number in case the pet has strayed from its owner), flea collars, toys, treats, grooming accessories, hygiene products, and pet training accessories. They are relatively low-involvement goods, and bundling to give savings and convenience to buyers is usually appreciated. They are also easy to prep for packaging to be fulfilled by Amazon, and not usually heavy to ship. If you have a great margin on this offering, consider to make your workload even easier by opting for Amazon to do the prep and labeling for you especially nearing the festive holidays. Opt for case packed items when shipping to Amazon fulfillment centers to benefit further from cheaper shipping costs and inventory placement fees.

4.3 Drop-shipping

Drop-shipping is permissible on Amazon on condition that the goods that are sent to the Amazon customer is prepped and labeled by the Amazon vendor, and does not contain any info of another e-commerce site. All customer-experiences must be handled directly by the vendor, including customer complaints, returns, and refunds.

Amazon specifies that drop-shipping is not permissible if the Amazon vendor acts merely as a middlemen function. Thus, it is also not an option for FBA-fulfillment, when goods have to be in the Amazon warehouses as inventory.

Drop-shipping is a lucrative way for Amazon vendors to make quick returns, bid for the buy box with competitive rates, or attract potential buyers to opt for their lower prices. Give caution to calculate that shipping costs are factored in, and shipping time should reflect accurately both the time the supplier is able to send the goods out, plus the time the supplier's partner will take to send the goods to the Amazon customer. Amazon customers are aware of the effort Amazon takes to ensure fast shipping, and great customer experience, thus disappointing in a promised delivery date might result in cancellations, and returns. Returns are very complicated with drop-shipping as specific information have to be submitted with the returns, shipment has to be paid by the vendor, and the supplier will usually charge a restocking fee. Returns usually happen when a customer is disappointed by the product that did not match the description or quality; but also if the size did not fit what they had expected would. Choose products for drop-shipping that avoid potential returns, and along with them bad reviews, as there is not much opportunity for a vendor to know the actual product they have bought before selling them at Amazon.

Enjoying your eBook so far? Take a moment to subscribe to our FREE newsletter for incredible discounts, books giveaways, and VIP offers!

> http://www.connectionbooksclub.com/bonus/

All we need is your email, and you'll be set up to receive more of the eBooks you can't wait to read.

4.4 Registering for Cashbacks

Many sourcing platforms attract third-party sellers to their platforms with cashback schemes. Cashback schemes are cash certificates rebated to a buyer for a percentage of what was spent on their site, much like a loyalty reward but in the form of cash that a buyer can use on the site for to save sourcing costs. Although cashbacks can take between one to three months to be rebated into the buyer's account, it will present some helpful extra cash in the long term that can help cushion buying costs of a product sourced on the same site.

Several sourcing sites have cashback schemes. Ebates, Swagbucks, Half.com, and Ebay Bucks are popular sites that Amazon FBA vendors have benefited from extra cash from cashbacks to help cushion a marketing or shipping budget. Some sites require a subscription which returns a higher cashback percentage for subscribers, that covers the subscription costs easily.

EXPERT TIP: Stacking is a method of sourcing that money-smart vendors use to earn savings while sourcing so that they have an advantage over competitors selling the same product. Using one or more of the following search sites, cashbackmonitor.com to search which shops offer cashbacks, and giftcardgranny.com to buy discounted gift cards. Take note also on an online store's promo code which may offer an added cashback when a purchase exceeds a certain amount. Together, this method of stacking together discounts can help reduce the price per unit cost of a product, so that a vendor gains a good buffer in profits when in a price war situation.

4.5 Managing your supply chain

Most likely, the product(s) that a vendor wishes to procure is available by many manufacturers. It is common to find resellers or agents who represent items of manufacturers, as they are able to communicate in ecommerce terms on the product to potential vendors. Identify if you would like to work through an agent or if you are able to work directly with the manufacturer.

When communicating with suppliers, vendors can take caution to achieve two types of information from the communications. The three lists below will achieve the first type of information, all about the product, and costing.

The product has to be completely compatible with what and how you intend to sell on Amazon FBA. Some important answers to get are:

- The size dimensions and weight of the product per unit, including their packaging, to ensure they fit in FBA's size criteria.
- The unit price, and minimum quantity order? This will give you the basic cost price of the product.
- What additional prep requirements might be required to ensure the product meets fulfillment prep requirements.
- How long does the supplier need to produce the order?
- How long does it take to ship to the fulfillment center?

The second set of questions may not relate to the product, but are of importance to ensure your competitive edge:

- Does the supplier have experience with vendors who sell on Amazon using FBA.
- Does the supplier sell directly on Amazon?
- What is the payment term?
- What is the return policy?
- What are the terms for defective items?
- What are the prices for reorders?
- What is the volume rebates?
- Which forwarding companies do they regularly use for shipment to fulfillment centers?
- Is the manufacturer able to affix labels on the packaging boxes for freight without extra costs?
- Is it possible to get a refund on sample purchases if an order is placed?
- Can the manufacturer hold 50 percent of the goods in their factory until the other has been sold?

EXPERT TIP: Rankings dip when a vendor's inventory runs low. While inventory is waiting to be replenished, the ratings drop and a vendor has to rerun the process of bringing up rankings when the stocks arrive. Having stock ready with a long-term supplier can manage this situation where products can be readily replenished without losing in ranking leverage. In some situations, manufacturers can partially finish a product, and work on other jobs until the vendor contacts them again to replenish the supply.

The third set of questions relate to any additional costs or additional work that the supplier might be required to do, or to recommend an affiliate:

- How can a vendor add their logo or private label on the product?
- Does the manufacturer have an in-house designer or a recommended partner who can assist with the labeling?
- Are there other products that the supplier may have that can make good bundle packages?
- What kind of product differentiation offering can be possible in the immediate or near future?

These questions will take a few days of communications to be answered. When retrieving answers, it can also help to conduct a bit of research on the supplier, their managers, and read reviews on them.

Sourcing for suppliers who can provide a long term and cost competitive product is essential for staying in the ecommerce business for the long run. Thus, the second type of questions, are inference questions to yourself: how long did the questions remain unanswered; was there a change of attitude through the communication process with difficult questions; were the questions constantly bounced off to different people in the company; do you have a gut feel that communication is not going to suit your work style? Before you commit financially or legally, reaching out to other suppliers is a prudent measure to ensure you will select the most effective supplier team.

EXPERT TIP: Identify those manufacturers who will have a good record in responding. Use a numbered list to order your questions, so that the vendor can answer all questions in an organised manner – this will also make it easier to collate the answers. Seek answers from as many suppliers as manageable who are supplying the product. Be open to ask questions to manufacturers that could give you an edge. Asking questions about the product beyond its advertised features may help a vendor to offer a more insightful bullet point description in your listing. Manufacturers are also aware of the importance of long-term relationships. They would like to build successful partnerships rather than one-time sales, and so may be willing to offer more insightful competition when sincerely approached.

Quite often, vendors overlook products manufactured in their own community, and use the convenience of online research. Buying locally means that there is a greater chance of cooperation, and a faster access to information and product knowledge.

Consider that the supplier is as important as your buyer, and that a healthy business relationship will be able to garner the support to meet the challenges that all businesses face. Thus, after a vendor has sufficient trust and dependency on a supplier, consider strategies on how to keep those suppliers happy so that your orders and competitive edge are in their considerations as well. Successful relationships are based on win-win formulas, and considering how suppliers will appreciate prompt payments, valuable positive and constructive feedback, polite management of challenging situations, clear instructions, and participation in the supplier objectives for certain product lines (perhaps in promotions, or less-exposed products) are ways in which a vendor can show sincere business support to a supplier quite easily.

EXPERT TIP: Like with any business, learn the specifications that make the product you are interested to sell truly unique. These are usually explained in industry jargon, or lingo, and differentiate the impression the manufacturer can have on your enquiries. When establishing new relationships, it is risky to partner with vendors who do not understand the product specifications, as it may suggest that the vendor will be unable to manage customers' questions or complains. Thus, if this language is not pre-learned, a vendor might lose the interest of the manufacturer.

EXPERT TIP: Amazon publishes on their website a Supply Chain Standard that lists some criteria that Amazon suppliers have to meet. It is useful to go through this list as a benchmark when selecting your supplier.

4.6 Ordering a Sample

It is important to order a sample prior to placing a large order. Samples can be easily paid with PayPal, and the sample costs are made up of the unit, customization cost, and freight cost. A sample is very important to use for product images required in the item listing. It is also important to test the sample for durability and quality – it should satisfy you before it goes into the market.

EXPERT TIP: Some manufacturers agree to refund the sample costs (excluding freight) to the vendor upon a large order.

4.7 Making Product Images

Ensure that the product is photographed from its packed stage including how it is sealed and presented, to its unpacking, and includes all the accessories. When taking product images, ensure that it is a professional photo of the product being sold. It must be in focus, against a pure white background, and must fill 85 per cent of the image frame. It should also be in an appropriate file format (TIFF, GIF, JPEG, or PNG), and must have image pixel dimensions of at least 1,000 or larger in either width or height, and be in a sRGB or CMYK color mode.

EXPERT TIP: Ensure that your file is saved in the exact format that Amazon wants, i.e. ASIN.format or UPC.format without exception. Ensure that the image file follows the product identifier (either the ASIN or UPC) followed by a period, and the file extension. Examples provided by Amazon include B000123456.jpg and 0237425673485.tif for reference. Ensure no spaces, dashes, or any additional characters are in the filename or the file will be rejected.

EXPERT TIP: Ensure that the product images are uploaded to Amazon's optimal specifications, so that customers are able to enlarge the images to view the product better.

4.8 Ordering barcodes

A vendor is required purchase barcodes if the product does not already have a UPC (or EAN for outside the US and Canada). A UPC is a 12-digit set of numbers that is a universally-used identifier for the product, in its description and packaging. If a vendor decides to create a private label or bundle of products, a separate UPC is required for that product offering.

A UPC will communicate the price to the customer, and upon sales, will communicate to the Point of Sale System (POS) of the store that the item has been sold, and is to be deleted from the inventory. It will also help to communicate with your reports on your revenue and your inventory.

There are several vendors to purchase UPCs including Amazon, eBay, Pacific Barcodes, and Avery. It is important that the barcodes are new and unused. Each UPC can be assigned to one offering, and cannot be reused for a different product offering. The barcodes are sent via in a text file via email, and can be in two formats: an EPS format, or an JPEG format. A vendor can pass the EPS format to the graphic illustrator to incorporate the barcode into the design of the packaging. With the JPEG format, it can be used on Word or Excel and printed with a laser inkjet printer, and easily printed on precut labels that are easily available in stationery stores.

EXPERT TIP: Ensure that you have all your product information and images available to input into the system when ordering new barcodes. When the barcodes are printed, test them with a barcode scanner App. Some popular Apps are Amazon Seller App, Scoutify, and Profit Bandit – many vendors use a combination of the Amazon App in combination with another professional App, as the Amazon App includes alerts for restricted products and access to the vendor's account.

4.9 Shipping the products to be fulfilled

Amazon has strict prepping criteria, and external packaging information that is required to run the supply chain smoothly. Ensure that your supplier is familiar which packing materials are not allowed, and how the shipment labels have to be made and placed. Alternatively, consider using a forwarder to go between your manufacturer and Amazon fulfillment centers. Ensure that the shipping labels are sent to your supplier or forwarder if the products are going to be delivered directly to Amazon fulfillment centers.

EXPERT TIP: Ensure that your shipments are packed optimally. Dimensional weight is calculated where items are charged by the size of the box they are packed in, rather than by their actual weight. This affects products that are light weight but bulky, and can be quite a substantial cost. Consider cutting down boxes to fit perfectly the product, or repackaging the product into smaller boxes that are of a more regular size, if possible. These additional costs add to your price per unit to be factored in when calculating if a product is going to give good profits.

EXPERT TIP: Ensure that your supplier has all the correct barcodes affixed to each unit, and the correct shipping label affixed to each external packaging. These are the common reasons why shipments do not get processed when they arrive. Working with an experienced FBA forwarder and manufacturer will help ensure that these common mistakes are picked out before they incur penalties from the fulfillment center. Some experienced FBA forwarders include FBAforward, and other vendors have used Middle Men strategies, where the shipment arrives at a freight forwarder or middle men, who inspects the products, manages any taxes and paperwork, provide extra prepping if required, and then reallocates the goods to the respective fulfillment warehouses.

Enjoying your eBook so far? Take a moment to subscribe to our FREE newsletter for incredible discounts, books giveaways, and VIP offers!

➢ http://www.connectionbooksclub.com/bonus/

All we need is your email, and you'll be set up to receive more of the eBooks you can't wait to read.

5. Selling on Amazon

When your item is finally in the FBA fulfillment warehouses, it will be listed as inventory for sale. Amazon is a highly competitive seller's platform, but there are many vendors who are successful, and can plan their strategies in line with the integrity concerns of Amazon that stipulates their regulations. Following are the eight expert tips a vendor can use to edge out a competitive market for their store.

6. EXPERT TIP #1: Write excellent listings

Mastering excellent listing skills is the first step into making a product visible on the Amazon platform. It is said that there are over 480 million products on the Amazon platform, thus excellent listing skills will ensure your product will be visible.

There are four main parts of a listing that buyers look out for: the title, the price, the images, and the reviews. An good listing will contain a good title and description that both gets found by the algorithm, and also convinces the buyer that the product is perfect for them. Together with high quality product images, and supportive reviews, these four parts of a listing are the main factors a vendor works with continuously to keep a competitive edge on the Amazon platform.

There are two areas on the listing page that requires the vendor to input product information: the product title, and the product description. Excellent listings incorporate keywords and product information in these two areas, so that the algorithm will pull out the product for buyers.

There are tools that can help a vendor plan which keywords to use when inputting the product's title. Such tools, e.g. Google AdWords Keyword Planner, keywordtool.io, Ubersuggest, and Soovle. It is also useful to take a look at competitors sites on Amazon to see which keywords they are using, especially those who own the Buy Box, and the Other Sellers.

A product title is usually given 200 characters, and of these characters, they should detail the product, and some specialized information that will set is apart from other generically-listed items. For example, when listing a headset, adding in the length of the cord, compatibility with specific products, and the size of the mini plug are all important at-a-glance information to interest a buyer looking for headsets. If the product is specific to a certain season or celebration, a title that says Easter brunch rabbit cake mold is more specific than cake mold will help pull your product along other buyers looking for Easter gifts or decorations.

EXPERT TIP: The stipulated number of characters include spaces and should be factored in when planning titles. The titles do not have to be grammatically perfect, that can be supplemented in the product description. Some fields of the listing will not be eligible for edits, thus be sure that the listing is excellently, and accurately written prior to posting, so as to prevent the possibility that the page has to be deleted and redone. Customers are able to report information on the listing that is misleading or untrue, so the information posted while aiming to be successful to be located in the keyword algorithm has to be accurate and honest towards the buyers.

A product description refers to the five bullet points that a vendor has to input to provide more information about the product. It gives a space of 500 characters, and no punctuation is required. Amazon has tailored these bullet points with the specific intention that it exemplifies fives benefits of fives features of the product. If the product has a warranty, or extra accessories, it should be listed as the last bullet. Thus, combining the considerations, a vendor can identify the main features or benefits of the product, organize the information, and rewrite the description with popular keywords.

EXPERT TIP: If there is ambiguity about the product being limited to work with certain models of complementary products only, consider to use a bullet point to list them so as to prevent buyers to complain, return, and write a bad review saying that the specifications were not clear. For example, a manufacturer may use the same design and color for producing colored mobile phone cables to both Android and iPhone users. A vendor who decides to sell only the product only compatible for iPhone users should specify in the description to be 'compatible only for iPhones only'. If an Android user did not realize that the product was made in two versions and as a result bought the incompatible cable, he or she will most likely issue a return and refund, thus resulting in unnecessary extra shipping and repackaging costs.

7. EXPERT TIP #2: Keep working on getting high rankings

- Use the correct merchant subscription.

There are two types of accounts for vendors on Amazon, an individual and a pro account. A pro account is designed and offered with the convenience that helps Amazon vendors be successful. It allows them to utilise their time effectively; it encourage sales with a decreasing transaction fee for a larger sales volume; it offers a larger range of products that Amazon only entrusts to reliable and professional vendors who have proven track records; and it collects invaluable Amazon-related data that are useful for sales, marketing, and product development.

Having a suitable merchant subscription makes the difference between being able to upload listings one at a time, or provide multiple listings in a collated manner; offer niche range products rather than products that are low-involvement and highly saturated with offers; and a lower cost per unit of product sold.

- Work on winning the Buy Box with good prices and excellent customer service.

When a vendor is a professional seller on Amazon, he is eligible to win the Buy Box and be the buy click button. Buy Box vendors are viewed highly by Amazon and assessed stringently. With high standards that please buyers, vendors who ensure that they are priced competitively, able to fulfill the products efficiently and cost-efficiently, and manage all customer concerns professionally are given the opportunity to win the buy box. This means performing better in all areas that matter to Amazon than one's competitors.

EXPERT TIP: Buy Box vendors are compliant with Amazon's A-Z Guarantee Claims and service standards. A-Z Guarantee Claims is the guarantee Amazon gives its customers to ensure them that they will back their buyers in times of conflict with vendors on their platform. This is a way Amazon tries to gain their trust and loyal following. Amazon recommends that vendors avoid matters coming into claims, and try to resolve all customer complaints with prompt feedback, refunds, and chargebacks promptly to minimize claims that Amazon has to take action on behalf of the buyer. Having many claims against a vendor reduces the chances of gaining the Buy Box.

8. EXPERT TIP #3: Create interesting and valuable bundles

A bundle is designed to create a new product offering that combines two or more items together. A bundle requires a new UPC, and while adding value in convenience and savings for the customer, usually also gives higher profitability to the vendors.

Reviews for successful bundles usually rave on the convenience and value in price that the bundle offered, and thus, these considerations determine what are the valuable bundles in Amazon's opinions. Amazon can remove bundle offerings that in their opinion are not complementary, or that are seen to have no intrinsic real value to the customers. Some bundles that can be seen on Amazon include instant cameras with photo albums, smart phone cases with styluses, replaceable toothbrush heads with toothpaste, and matching notebooks and pens. Vendors tend to get creative with bundles and when reciprocated with appreciative buyers, can generate good reviews.

There are guidelines on bundling policies on Amazon, for example that media is only allowed as a complimentary related product in a bundle. Other than that, bundles can contain products from different categories, but they must be complementary products that are good value for customers.

Bundles are listed as a product offering that can only be bought together, and thus have their own unique barcode, and listing page. It is unusual that identical bundles will be offered, thus it is likely that this bundle will have little competition and thus, higher probability of sales. It is important that the product title contains the word 'bundle' and when possible, lists the items that are part of the bundle. The product image must only have the actual images from the products in the bundle and not other resembling or unoffered items. The bundle must be listed in the category of its highest-costing product, except if the product is a media product, upon which it should be listed in the category of its second highest-costing product, as media cannot be listed as a main product offering in a bundle.

Multipacks, not to be confused with bundles, are multiple numbers of the same product, i.e. that have the identical barcode. If a product is offered in two different colors, that would not be a multipack, but would be a bundle. Multipacks also have their unique UPC and be packed as a single product offering, that cannot be separated throughout the fulfillment process.

EXPERT TIP: Products that are bundle offerings must be prepped as a single package. It has to have its own barcode on the packaging that can be easily scanned, and it must have a label that states it is a bundle and should not be separated. Ensure that products are first individually packed as per their prep requirements, and then again packed together as a single bundle offering with their unique barcode.

Enjoying your eBook so far? Take a moment to subscribe to our FREE newsletter for incredible discounts, books giveaways, and VIP offers!

> ➤ http://www.connectionbooksclub.com/bonus/

All we need is your email, and you'll be set up to receive more of the eBooks you can't wait to read.

9. EXPERT TIP #4: Excite buyers with creative marketing strategies

The sure way to excite buyers as an Amazon vendor, is to offer a raved-about product, at a lower than usual price, and within a certain period only. Vendors who set up a product and leave it to work for itself with a lukewarm ad campaign, seldom excite buyers. On the other hand, vendors who constantly keep a vibe alive around their products, and who have constantly reviews by excited users create an excitement around their product, so that curious people just have to buy one to experience what the buzz was about.

Reviews are the most effective word-of-mouth way to get buyers curious and excited. Most successful vendors use reviewers both within the Amazon ecosystem, and from the social media world. There are more restrictions on how a vendor may procure a review from Amazon buyers and reviewers, but the veteran buyers have expressed benefitting from these new measures as they have reduced the number of short-term opportunists-competing vendors, and as well have resulted in buyers being more willing to provide organic and genuine reviews as they feel less harassed.

There is a two-step process on how a vendor can excite a buyer. First, the vendor needs to excite the reviewers. Then, the vendor needs to make the buy exciting for the client through limited time value-for-money. In effect, it requires a vendor to excite two groups of people with her product.

It is important to reach out to reviewers who are professionals. Professional reviewers take their jobs seriously. They could be doing reviews as a part-time job, but still put in many equal hours a week to review products. They usually are not bound by a certain medium, meaning they probably have their own website, their own blog, are part of a social media-based review group, and write eloquently and professionally. They use neutral language to communicate, research what features are important for a buyer regarding such a product, focus on product aspects that buyers who cannot experience the product prior to buying are most concerned about. These aspects include packaging, durability, quality, and other charming or interesting aspects for the product that can be valuable for either a niche group or then a broader audience. Professional reviewers are very highly sought-after: they have their honest opinions (which are well valued by the buyers); they personalise in their review categories and may not participate in a wide range of products; they prefer to work in the buyers' interests than the vendors'; they are willing to spend money to procure products to review (being professionals they are aware that Amazon policy does not permit free products in return for positive reviews); and they are easy to locate, but may be already very busy with offers by other vendors and organisations who are using (and perhaps paying for) their review services.

EXPERT TIP: While organic reviews are important, professional reviews often communicate in a more insightful, and accurate writing style. They usually also leave out personal opinions. Ideally, the professional reviewer is a potential target audience of your product. Amazon Vine Program or Vine Voices are an example of a professional review group. Reviewers are invited by Amazon by invitation, and choose the products they wish to review. They are also assessed on their ability as a professional reviewer, and their reviews are usually top of the product review list and identified with a badge. When a vendor subscribes for the review program, it gives a lifetime review, and is a good long-term investment return for a product that will continue to sell itself on the Amazon platform.

As with the emphasis on maintaining good relationships with customers and manufacturers, maintaining a professional relationship with reviewers is often an under-explored marketing aspect of running a successful online business. Selling via ecommerce removes an essential customer experience and service from the customer. Reviewers provide that service for buyers. It helps buyers make educated choices much like a property agent or a sales agent at a shoe shop might.

EXPERT TIP: Seek professional reviewers through social review groups on social media. These reviewers usually participate in a group they identify with, either on a geographic, psychometric, or demographic basis, and will be directly relevant to your product's targeted audience. Tomoson, Buview, and Zonblast are some independent website that a vendor can use to access reviewers.

With the written marketing ideas taken care of by reviewers, vendors can also look towards using Instagram to reach the audience who are more interested in visual impressions of a product, than written reviews. Working like how ads in a glossy magazine entice a buyer, Instagram allows a vendor to go beyond the white background product image restrictions of Amazon, to entice potential buyers on short messages, and great images. It is relatively uncomplicated for a vendor who is already using Instagram socially. A vendor who is trying out Instagram for the first time just needs to keep in mind how to phrase hashtags, how to keep a regular appearance with scheduled postings, and to create an element of fun in the campaign. Keep to tangible goals that convert to buys for your product. Great Instagram posts that feature products often include fun-based images, videos of the product in use, and other useful bits of interesting information that is not only business-related to sales, as they try to create an environment around their product.

EXPERT TIP: Vendors use a combination of Facebook and Instagram features to cross-promote their product. They also include links that easily leads the viewer to their product page. This is very effective as opposed to the viewer going into Amazon to conduct a search and sieving through the competitors.

To convert interested customers into buying customers, consider using the oldest trick in the book: promotions. Creating excitement for buyers, and from which most people have happy experiences about, makes the buy a great value. Great values indicate not only a price savings. They also refer to incentivized buys, for example, loyalty discounts, free product samples or free gifts, and they all leverage on the value being earned by a call-to-action limited time offer. These relate happy experiences to the buyer (think of a child buying a magazine for the attractive free toy that comes with it), and are proven successful ways to get a customer's attention. They can be just straightforward offers, or paired with interactive contests for customers to share their voice by sending in photos or participating in quizzes. The fun factor of such contests reflect back on the community using the vendor's product, and begin to create a following that can be used as inferred reviews, and happy customers.

EXPERT TIP: Be sure to return the attention that your followers on Instagram give you. Successful vendors know that healthy relationships are two-way, that translates into the seller also being interested in the customer. See if you can convert these followers into a database of customers from which you can implement targeted campaigns for, and who will be happy to receive news and updates from you. These people however will need to see a value add in terms of incentives, value buys, discounts, coupons, free gifts, great advice, a fun community, and reciprocal interests in them in order to continue participating in your campaign group. It is key to remember that although marketing activities are taken outside Amazon, these people are usually Amazon customers, and so keeping them happy is right in line with creating value to Amazon's customer policy.

10. EXPERT TIP #5: Manage your reviews professionally

A successful Amazon vendor can set himself apart from his competition by managing reviews professionally. Treat all reviews as constructive comments. Most good reviews will also contain a little constructive comment that vendors can use as opportunities to develop good relationships with their buyers.

EXPERT TIP: It is possible to create message templates on your Amazon seller account to address questions that either trigger reviews, or address review topics before hand. Designed as standard answers to frequently asked questions, message templates allow a vendor to manage buyer expectations by answering in advance any questions that relates to the product, shipping, quality, or sizing. Most buyers apart from looking at the images and reviews will also study the FAQs before purchasing a product. Designing questions on the product's fit, for example, stating that the size will run a little small, or a little big, will help the buyer make a better size decision. If reviews come in that the sizes are not as they had thought to be, it is convenient either for another reviewer or the vendor to reply that it was mentioned to be so in the FAQs. In effect, it is another method for a vendor to communicate effectively with potential buyers to increase the chances of positive customer experiences.

Potential buyers who are reading reviews also look out for how these reviews were received. If a vendor shows interests to resolve the matter, and provides sufficient reasonable explanations for the mistake, it is likely that the attitude of resolving the matter outshines the problem itself. Participate in the conversation either on the thread, or with the reviewer directly, and strive to resolve the disappointment. It is usual that bad reviews are taken back by the reviewer when the matter has been resolved. Some vendors provide contact information on the package itself, for example, an email address the customer can contact if they are unsatisfied with the product, so a dissatisfied customer usually will use that method to contact the vendor directly rather than posting a complaint through the Amazon page. It helps to give the vendor an opportunity and some time to resolve the problem directly without going through the reviews or complaints page of Amazon.

EXPERT TIP: Although bad reviews are not possible to be removed, identify characteristics of the bad reviews that may be in violation of Amazon posting regulations, for example, if they contain obscene language, threats, or defamatory information. Much like the regulations in place to ensure vendors are professional, there are regulations in place on how buyers must behave in reviews. If a negative review is inaccurate in the matter they complain about, or contain disturbing comments, and if they lead to an uncomfortable information sharing environment, it is possible to request Amazon's help to make the site more professional and friendly.

It takes an effort of an organic buyer to leave an organic review. Successful Amazon vendors usually thank their reviewers for this effort, and use this opportunity to develop a conversation with their customers and include them in future promotions that will add value to them, for example, an invite to a 24 hours only sale that has limited stock. While it is important to look after the disappointment customers, it is equally important to keep the satisfied customers continuously appreciated. Some vendors communicate this importance to their buyers by including the QRCode in the product box that be easily scanned with their smart phones so that it is made even more convenient for the customer to leave a review without having to get to a computer.

EXPERT TIP: Professional sites like feedbackfive.com help to send emails to actively solicit feedback from buyers. It also opens an avenue for dissatisfied customers to contact the vendor directly to solve the problem. Being alert to these potential negative reviews can help a vendor actively reduce negative reviews, and also improve customer satisfaction as most reviewers are willing to remove their negative feedback when they are being addressed fairly.

EXPERT TIP: It is advisable to remove the Default Repackaging option for returned products in order to be sure all the parts are returned, and as well, assess the complain of the customer. Review the product quality and faults brought up by the buyer, and observe if similar complains and returns occur for the same reasons. These are important observations to bring up to the manufacturer and reevaluate important product decisions before more complains come in. Using negative reviews constructively will lead to better skills in managing conflicts and complains both with the customers and the suppliers, that when managed with positively and responsibly, will turn a challenging situation into a positive experiences for the stakeholders.

11. EXPERT TIP #6: Work with professional tools to increase sales

Like any serious business, Amazon vendors use a variety of professional tools to advertise their product, and to identify if they have a market share or a leading edge in their online store. These tools usually require an advertising budget, but the following tips can help maximize the returns on investment, and to ensure that the information retrieved from these tools can be converted into better sales and marketing performances.

- Determine if you can reach your target audience with the tools.

Different tools use different algorithms to arrive at a specific group of audience. If a vendor's products are all in the same category, or if it caters to a specific target audience, e.g. diet-conscious men, then the tools will be utilized differently to arrive at the desired data collation.

Most vendors would begin with Amazon Sponsored Ads, or Amazon Pay Per Click (PPC). Ensure that your product is in a category that is supported by Amazon Ads if you would like to use PPC as a main marketing tool to increase sales. Amazon Ads can be easily activated via Amazon Seller Central at "Campaign Manager" with automatic targeting. It is easily planned with a daily budget, and some vendors select automatic targeting, while others prefer manual targeting. The minimum daily budget for the campaign on Amazon Pay Per Click is $1, and the minimum default bid is $0.05. Vendor advertisers are only charged when they have the buy box, so the cost of advertising is directly related to the conversion rate of purchases from a genuine buyer.

EXPERT TIP: It is important not to set up a campaign and then forget about it. The ad campaign is most effective when implemented and analyzed with its reports. Reports show how many views on the product occurred, versus what the conversion rate was. When the views are high, but conversion rate is low, and customers are buying from a stronger competitor, this can be a call for promoting the product with a lower price.

Facebook Ads allow the advertiser to reach a targeted audience by filtering data by country, state, city, and even down to the zip code, if your product is going to be relevant to people for a specific location. Such campaigns can work for bird houses designed for specific birds that are native to a particular location who are promoting protection for the species. Another example could be for products that are available on Amazon pantry – such campaigns thus can be focused only on zip codes where Amazon pantry is available in. Some vendors may also wish to reach audiences through psychometric profiling to reach specific gender, age, religious, hobby, or interests groups.

EXPERT TIP: To set up a Facebook ad, log into your Facebook account, and click on 'Create an Ad'. Facebook has a section on the ad planning 'Plan' has two kinds of information for a new advertiser: 'Audience Insights' and 'Creative Hub'. Audience Insights provide demographic breakdowns that can help an advertiser get a targeted audience. Creative Hub is a collection of possible ad campaigns that a beginner with Facebook Ads can experiment with. There are four main categories of campaigns: interactive, video, image, and Instagram, and they are filled with inspiring videos. A guiding Mockup tool gives the potential advertiser a clear format to create mock campaigns, and experiment with the message, look, and feel of the campaign all within the tool.

Another professional tool used by Amazon vendors is Google AdWords. Adwords can work with Search Ads or Display Ads. This campaign works with keyword searches as opposed to demographic profiling, and Google AdWords has a free keyword tool that helps to locate the most popular keywords related to your product.

Some vendors choose to use banner ads and video ads to promote on YouTube. Advertising on YouTube allows an advertiser to choose if they wish to reach the entire YouTube.com audience, or a particular channel or video that is most likely to show your ad to your potential buyer. As YouTube is a browsing portal in itself, and contains a large stock of videos that can distract your buyer, it is useful to include a call to action within your ad, and use concise words and outstanding features that will catch and hold the viewers' attention.

EXPERT TIP: Some vendors are hesitant to master social media marketing, and after the successful launch of a campaign, tend to slow down and not deal with it longer. It is often considered as a project, or a campaign, like it is named. However, a successful product requires constant reminder campaigns to the buyers why it is good. Most vendors do set aside a budget from profits to fund new campaigns for the same product. A good, valuable product that has been the result of careful attention to managing supplier, Amazon, and customer relationships can be self-running. However, for this product to be running in the forefront of the buyers' thoughts, frequent campaigns have to be maintained.

- You product relies on your product images to make the conversion rate.

Veteran Amazon sellers know that uploading many great product images is key to make a sale. It helps give more information about a product, and develops trust with the potential buyer to choose a vendor over another. It also helps give confidence to the quality and condition of the product.

Amazon gives a vendor a specific format for the photo files, and the ability to upload up to nine photo images. These images can be updated even if the product is already listed, and takes 24 hours to refresh to the updated images. A main product image is the most important photo for the product that gives the look and feel of the product. Up to eight other images can show the product in its various angles, showcase special features, give a feel for the size and texture of the product, or promote a lifestyle look and feel of the product using models. Images on how the product is packaged is important as it shows how well packed the product will be when it arrives, and is useful for purchases intended as gifts.

Although only certain Amazon vendors can upload videos, using cross-channel social media marketing can allow you to use videos to promote your Amazon product, and link back to your Amazon listing page for sales.

- Set a clear goal.

Set a goal in terms of how many units you would like to sell, and by when. This is important to manage a product's actual cost, and the results of a campaign. If the goal is to sell a thousand products, assess if those results were reached within the time frame you have allocated for the campaign. There is storage costs for the inventory sitting in the fulfillment centers, and the campaign should move the products so that they are not incurring extra storage costs especially during peak seasons. It should also give clear data that helps to plan for restocking inventory to meet the demand, and also to fill the inventory for the next campaign.

- Be disciplined not to spend above your ad budget.

It is easy to be tempted to launch a few campaigns at a time and over a few platforms in the hope of getting a large audience. This however translates into higher costs. Having a higher budget will help reach a larger audience, but it may not convert into a buying audience, and nor may a vendor have sufficient stock to meet the immediate demand in the short term.

Consider the costs that the ad campaign(s), and be sure to include those costs against your profit margins. For example, if a campaign is going to cost $1,000 and there are only 200 units of products available for sale, $5 dollars has to be added into each unit cost to reflect an accurate profit for the product. Factor in also that the products can take a few months for manufacturing and shipping, and consider if the ad dollars spent can still be effective when the product is back in inventory.

EXPERT TIP: AdWords will ask that every ad campaign have its keywords, landing page, and text, so these are important information to research on prior to spending on ad campaigns.

- Use the data from the campaigns to study how to improve your product listing

It is very important to study the reports generated from the ad campaign to study how potential buyers are reacting to your product. These reports study the ACoS and conversion rates between impressions (people who view the ad), and actual buyers. Not receiving enough impressions can be a question about keyword relevance or budget issues, but low conversion rates can also mean that the campaign was not optimally launched. It is important to study which part of the four factors of the listing may need improvement, and if the product is relevant to the people it has reached out to.

- Set aside sufficient time

There are three factors of timing to consider with an ad campaign. There first is allowing the campaign to run between a week to two weeks in order to get some reliable patterns to analyze. Pulling a campaign only after a couple of days cannot give accurate results on how the product is actually being received.

The second is to ensure that the momentum built from the campaign does not end abruptly when the sales roll in. Continuous advertising is required to keep the product and brand in the buyer's mind, thus some vendors who take down a campaign find that they have to rebuild the momentum again when promoting the same product.

Lastly, set aside sufficient time to conduct extensive research on the keywords required to make the product visible to a buyer who is seeking it.

Enjoying your eBook so far? Take a moment to subscribe to our FREE newsletter for incredible discounts, books giveaways, and VIP offers!

> http://www.connectionbooksclub.com/bonus/

All we need is your email, and you'll be set up to receive more of the eBooks you can't wait to read.

12. EXPERT TIP #7: Observe Trademarks

The trademarks in this tip does not refer to the brand products that are protected from gated categories. These trademarks refer to protected images, phrases, and designs that are filed with Amazon. Amazon posts its own listing of trademarks on the site that 'Non-Exhaustive List of Amazon Trademarks'. This list contains phrases 'Apply & Buy' and 'BEFORE YOU BUY' and product listings that use these trademarked phrases will be taken down from the Amazon listings.

Ensure that your listings and products do not infringe upon trademarks as this can cause a hold on the account or a removal of listing, that can hurt sales.

EXPERT TIP: Trademarks are applied to class, and a vendor will need to prove that the trademark used is not in violation because it does not infringe upon sales of the trademarked product in the same category.

13. EXPERT TIP #8: Understand your tax obligations

It is important for Amazon vendors to be savvy on their tax liabilities as a business on Amazon so that they are not using profits to pay fines. There are two types of taxes that an Amazon vendor will face with each transaction made, i.e. income tax, and sales tax. Income tax touches on a vendor's merchant-fulfilled sales, FBA sales, shipping credits, gift-wrap credits, and promotional rebates. All of these figures relate to how much a vendor declares as income, and how much taxes are paid for the activities on Amazon. Sales taxes affect only taxes on sales, shipping, and gift-wrap services that a buyer pays for.

EXPERT TIP: Amazon Professional Sellers who have made more than $20,000 in gross, unadjusted sales, or have conducted more than 200 transactions, are obligated to report their income through a self-service interview process available on the Amazon Seller Central, who in turn send this information to the IRS (File Form 1099-K). Gross unadjusted sales include sales that have been returned, damaged, or refunded, so it is important to report these statistics accurately. If a vendor has multiple seller accounts but with a same Tax Identification Number (TIN), the sales must be collated into one single filing rather than multiple filling. Ensure that there are no misspellings when filing as this can cause the filing to be unsucessful, and thus subject to tax liabilities.

Sales taxes are described as pass-through sales. The vendor does not get to keep these taxes, but collect them on behalf of the state, and transfer the money to the state either in monthly, quarterly, or annual cycles. Sales taxes are mandatory in almost all US states are considered to a funding resource for government projects. Sales taxes affects an Amazon vendor when there is an office or home office in a state; if there are employees in a state; and if there is inventory stored in a state.

There are a few matters that an Amazon FBA vendor needs to clarify. First, is the product liable to be taxed. If the product is taxable, they then need to know how much tax is levied on the product. Next, a vendor needs to identify the states in which they have nexus in. Nexus refers to a business presence that a vendor has in the state. FBA vendors need to be informed that shipments sent to fulfillment centers do not reflect accurately where the goods are further redirected to after being processed for fulfillment. There are at the moment about 15 Amazon fulfillment centers. A search through a vendor's reports will be able to locate the exact fulfillment centers where a vendor's inventory is stored. If this search proves challenging, there are tools that veteran FBA sellers use to manage their taxes efficiently, e.g. TaxJar, or Taxify amongst others. These tools not only help locate nexus status for present and past transactions, but also include information on how much taxes need to be collected and remitted to the state authorities. They require a subscription usually, but have been raved about as great time savers.

Each state has its own sales tax criteria and sales tax rate, and some states divide it further to each local district. Some states require tax rates to be origin-based, and others destination-based. Understanding where sales activities or business presence occur can help an FBA seller determine the sales taxes that are due to the local state. Prior to collecting taxes, a vendor is required to apply for a license, and the process can take between two to three hours. If business activity has ceased in a state, a final filing of sales tax returns to the state is necessary to stipulate that the business will not have continued presence in the state, so that the costs of maintaining the license, and obligations to file for taxes will be recorded to be discontinued.

EXPERT TIP: Vendors are required to apply for a license before collecting sales taxes from buyers. It is criminal to collect sales taxes without a valid license.

EXPERT TIP: There are sales tax holidays that are worth noting. One is usually at the beginning of a school year where no taxes are levied on students needs to buy school materials. Another is prior to the start of hurricane season where people are not levied on taxes for the goods they need to stock up to tie through the hurricane damage. A vendor whose account is set up to collect sales taxes must remember not to collect sales taxes for these categories of goods during this period, and accurate receipts of sales must be submitted when filing for income or sales taxes.

Enjoying your eBook so far? Take a moment to subscribe to our FREE newsletter for incredible discounts, books giveaways, and VIP offers!

> ➢ http://www.connectionbooksclub.com/bonus/

All we need is your email, and you'll be set up to receive more of the eBooks you can't wait to read.

14. EXPERT TIP #9: Speak the lingo

Many Amazon sellers communicate in forums, blogs, and produce videos to share information with each other. Understanding the acronyms that are used daily and commonly will go a long way to help follow the threads, and participate in the conversation. Here are some acronyms and phrases that are most commonly used between vendors on Amazon.

Amazon-related terms and acronyms

ASIN - Amazon Standard Identification Number; **FBA** - Fulfillment by Amazon; **FNSKU** - Fulfillment Network Stock Keeping Unit; **HBA** - Health and Beauty Aids; **MF** - Merchant Fulfill; **FBM** - Fulfillment By Merchant; **MFN** - Merchant Fulfilled Network; **SC** - Seller Central; **A9** - a company of Amazon that is dedicated to product, visual, and cloud search; **Amazon API** - a web service that gives application programmers access to Amazon's product catalog data; **GTIN** - Global Trade Item Number; **WL** - White Label, i.e. selling an existing product with a vendor's own brand; **PL** - Private Label, i.e. selling a customized product; **BSR** - Best Sellers Rank; **BMVD** - Book, Movie, Video, & DVD; **GL** - Gated List; **MSKU** - Merchant Stock Keeping Unit; **Brand Registry** - a program offered by Amazon for sellers to register and protect their brand with Amazon; **Buy Box** - the actual listing a buyer sees of a product that the buyer wishes to buy; **Gated Category or Restricted Category**; **Lightning Deals** - a promotion where a limited number of products are offered at a discount for a short period of time; **Vendor Express** - vendors with whom Amazon buy their products from; **Verified review** - a review made by an buyer of the product; **BB Seller** - Buy Box Seller;

Stores

AZ/AMZ - Amazon; **BL** - Big Lots; **BM** - Brick and Mortar Store; **TRU** - Toys R Us; **Wags/WAG** - Walgreens; **WM** - Walmart; **TG** - ThinkGeek; **BAM** - Books-A-Million; **BN** - Barnes & Noble; **T** - Target; **TJM** - TJ Maxx;

Business Terms

BOGO - Buy One Get One; **BOLO** - Be on Look Out; **BTS** - Back to School; **COGS** - Cost of Goods Sold; **EAN** - European Article Number; **ISBN** - International Standard Book Number; **MAP** -

Minimum Advertised Price; **MSRP** - Manufacturer's Suggested Retail Price; **OA** - Online Arbitrage; **OTC** - Over the Counter; **Q1** - Quarter 1, i.e. 1 January to 31 March of; **Q2** - Quarter 2, i.e. 1 April to 30 June; **Q3** - Quarter 3, i.e. 1 July - 30 September; **Q4** - Quarter 4, i.e. 1 October - 31 December; **RA** - Retail Arbitrage; **Replen** - Replenishable item; **ROI** - Return on Investment; **UPC** - Universal Product Code; **YMMV** - Your Mileage May Vary; **WS** - Wholesale buying; **DS** - Dropshipping; **PM** - Profit Margin; **EIN** - Employee Identification Number; **CB** - Cashback; **KC** - Kohls Cash; **GC** - Gift Card; **CC** - Credit Card; **SKU** - Stock Keeping Unit; **ASP** - Average Sales Price; **BF** - Black Friday; **FTFBA** - Full-Time FBA; **LTH** - Long-term Hold; **LTSF** - Long-term Storage Fees; **OOS** - Out of Stock; **TA** - Tactical Arbitrage; **TM** - Tuesday Morning; **WA** - Wholesale Arbitrage; **ATOP** - At time of posting; **FB** - Facebook; **HTF** - Hard to find; **TIA** - Thanks in Advance; **VA** - Virtual Assistant

Apps and Professional Tools: **IL** - Inventory Lab; **OAX** - OA Xray; **CCC** - CamelCamelCamel; **PB** - Profit Bandit; **SM** - Scanner Monkey; **SP** - Scan Power;

15. EXPERT TIP #10: Use professional Amazon FBA tools

Finally, the last expert tip to share: Use professional tools designed for the Amazon FBA seller. An Amazon vendor typically uses savvy tools to get ahead of game, and there are many professional tools designed by vendors for vendors. They cover every aspect of the vendor experience from identifying products to marketing strategies. Here are some professional tools outside the Amazon-developed tools that have worked well for successful Amazon vendors. Most Amazon vendors will use a combination of Amazon tools (Amazon Seller App, FBA Calculator, Volume Listing Tools) and other subscription-based subscription tools to suit the challenge or focus they have on hand.

For tools that aid ratings: feedbackexpress.com; feedbackgenius.com; feedbackfive.com; bqool.com; salesbacker.com; convertkit.com;

For tools that aid inventory management: teikametrics.com; inventorylab.com; stitchlabs.com; automcf.com; selleractive.com;

For tools that aid listings and pricing advice: neatoscan.com; repricerexpress; scanpower; sellerengine; inventorylab.com; cleerplatinum.com; merchantwords.com; adwords.google.com; amzsecrets.com; keywordinspector.com;

For tools that aid scanning: asellertool.com; scoutify app;

For tools that aid procuring: howmanyextension.com; profitsourcery.com; junglescout.com; trends.google.com; jumpsend.com;

For services that aid financing: kabbage.com;

For shipping service: shipworks.com

For tools that aid taxes: taxjar.com

For receiving payments from international markets: currenciesdirect.com

For services that aid customer service: groovehq.com;

For tools that aid product images and artwork: upgradedimages.com; fiverr.com; canva.com;

EXPERT TIP: Use the free trial periods to test the tools before subscribing. Not all tools will suit every operating system, and it is very important that reports generated from these tools will be converted readily into easily understandable data for a vendor to utilize effectively. There are many videos available online that will review these tools, and are worth researching on prior to paying subscriptions. As the Amazon tools are free for professional sellers, it is useful to see what functions lack in these tools, before seeking out the tool that will best meet your short and long term objectives.

Conclusion

We hope that you have benefitted from the tips from this book. The Amazon seller environment is constantly staying vigilant to uphold the policies that Amazon holds dear to maximize its customers' experiences, and to be at the forefront as a consumer's e-commerce solution. As such, it has created many opportunities for people who normally would hold day jobs, into becoming full-time e-commerce vendors. There is market space for arbitrage vendors, individual sellers, and professional sellers. Best practices help advise vendors to stay maintain healthy Amazon seller accounts, access gated and restricted categories, and benefit long-term by providing creative and valuable products and services to Amazon customers, and to Amazon. As regulations are regularly implemented to promote even better buyer experiences, and restrictions towards sellers also regularly enforced to weed out less-pleasant vendors to deal with, be sure to look out for our upcoming edited versions of the book to be well informed of the best tips and advice for Amazon FBA sellers, so that you can make the best unique value proposition for your store. Bye for now!

Thank you!!!
Can I ask
a favor?

I see you've made it all the way to the end of my book. Thank you so much for reading my book. I'm so glad you enjoyed it enough to get all the way through!

As you probably know, many people look at the reviews on Amazon before they decide to purchase a book.

If you liked the book, would you be open to leaving me a 4 or 5 star review?

You see, I'm a self published author, and when people like you are able to give me reviews, it helps me out in a big way.

60 seconds is all I'm asking for, and it would mean the world to me. You can leave a review for me in the amazon.com site.

It'd really mean a lot to me.

Thank you so much,

Robert Hawthorn

More Great Books By This Author

amazon FBA

This book will introduce you to the most effective strategies for getting your Amazon FBA business off the ground. Even as a novice seller, you will be introduced to the principles that will put you a step ahead of the competition. Learn the secrets of the trade – don't make beginner's mistakes. Get informed on everything from packaging logistics to legal know-how. This book covers:

- Essentials of retail arbitrage
- How to start your private label
- The best marketing strategies for improving reviews and sales
- Effective shipping and inventory management
- How to find profitable products to sell
- Making the most of Amazon FBA tools
- How to register a business and deal with tax issues

From guiding principles to the day-to-day details, this guide goes in depth to explain the ins and outs of the most successful company in the world and how you can become a part of it. With a proper introduction, you will be ready to put an unbeatable business plan into action. Avoid the pitfalls of going in blind and get equipped to handle the thrills and challenges of selling. Amazon FBA offers the advantage of markets across the world, and this book serves as your guide to making the most of it.

PASSIVE INCOME ONLINE

Do you try and try to scrimp and save money but still finding yourself coming up a little short when you really need it? The good news if you start your own online business even if you are a beginner. You have the potential of generating a passive income online stream that will help you meet and exceed your financial goals this book is the right guide for you. If you are interested in learning more about all the hottest streams, then Passive Income: 20 Ideas and Strategies to Start an Online Business That Make a Passive Income for You Every Day is the book you have been waiting for.

Here you will find the top 20 Ideas for investing your money to maximize 100% of your profits, including all the tips and TRICKS!

Inside you will find nearly 2 dozen passive income generating ideas, many of them with the ability to start generating real results in as little as a few hours!! You don't need to wait more than 90 days, or 30 days, you can start doing it and receiving money today!

Here you will find the top 20 Ideas for life! Investing your money to maximize 100% of your profits, including all tips and TRICKS! You will be able to work less and earn more!

The passive income scenarios described inside this book take all shapes and sizes including website creation, content creation, aggregation and propagation and even simply letting Google and other companies keep an eye on your data. Forget all the myths about online passive income that you may have heard about, the one thing that is for sure is: if you are interested in passive income then there is a lot of ways to do it, and you can choose the ones that most fits your lifestyle and become financially free.

Inside you will find

- How to invest in real estate for as little as $50
- The easiest ways to make money from social media
- The best passive income stream for those with no startup capital
- And much, much more.

Go ahead and Enjoy it!

PASSIVE INCOME ONLINE

20 Ideas and Strategies to Start an Online Business
That Make a Passive Income for You Every Day

ROBERT C. HAWTHORN

Have you ever wished that you were better with money?

Do you ever find yourself being overwhelmed by the state of your personal finances?

Would you like to become more financially responsible?

Now you can, with 5 Reasons to Invest in Money Management: Learn How to Organize Your Financial Life and Invest in Your Future, a short self-help book that is packed with information on how to make the most of your financial situation.

If you want to be able to lower your interest rates, learn up to date money management strategies and turn your financial situation into one of prosperity and stability, then you'll find the answers inside, with solid advice that includes:

- ✔ Strategies which are designed for the average person
- ✔ Your options for retirement
- ✔ Hacks for navigating the grocery store's subtle spending traps
- ✔ Ways to pay less than you owe on credit cards and other outstanding debts
- ✔ Finding freedom with financial stability

Suitable for complete novices, 5 Reasons to Invest in Money Management is a book that will transform the way you look at and deal with your finances.

Download copy and start investing in your future today! Prosperity is waiting for YOU!

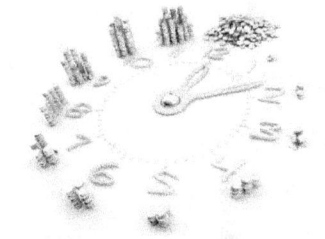

MONEY
MANAGEMENT

Learn how to organize your financial life and invest in your future.

ROBERT C HAWTHORN

PUBLIC SPEAKING

Would you like to improve your public speaking skills but don't know how?

Would you like to be better prepared for public speaking engagements?

Public speaking is an art. It requires skill, practice and a certain degree of nerve to be able to stand in front of an audience and deliver a good speech which is interesting and entertaining.

That's why, in just 10 chapters, **Public Speaking: Ways You Can Improve Your Public Speaking**, gives you pertinent and useful information which will improve your performance and increase your confidence, and includes:

- ✓ Understanding the basics
- ✓ Using your emotions effectively
- ✓ Gestures and expressions to help get your point across
- ✓ What the audience wants
- ✓ Dealing with the dreaded stage fright
- ✓ Maintaining speech rhythm
- ✓ And much more…

Learning how to overcome your fears, negative experiences and dealing with questions efficiently are all part of becoming a great public speaker.

And with **Public Speaking** you have the ideal resource which you can read from cover to cover or simply pick and choose the parts which you feel are most relevant.

Get yourself a copy today! Becoming a better public speaker is within your grasp.

PUBLIC SPEAKING

ROBERT C HAWTHORN

PUBLIC SPEAKING

Ways You Can Improve Your Communications Skills

ROBERT C HAWTHORN

NETWORK MARKETING

Network marketing is quickly becoming one of the most efficient and effective ways to earn a livable income from your own home! Many people dream about becoming their own boss, but so few actually take action. The thought of investing your time and money into starting your own business can be daunting. But this guide of the network marketing industry will teach you what you need to know about the business, and how to become the envied success story that others hear about.

In this book you will learn:

- ✔ The Basic Psychology of Network Marketing
- ✔ Becoming the Ideal Salesman
- ✔ Opportunities vs. Scams
- ✔ Product Promotion and Advertisement
- ✔ People Management and Team Building
- ✔ Finding Motivation and Making the Final Sale
- ✔ Communication is Key
- ✔ Keeping Your Eyes on the Competition
- ✔ Building a Steady Income
- ✔ Understanding taxes

It is time to take action and gain control of your life. You can live the life of your dreams and manage a successful career in which you are the boss. Network marketing is the ideal opportunity to become financially stable and make money doing something that you really love.

NETWORK MARKETING

A BEGINNER'S GUIDE FOR A SUCCESSFUL NETWORK MARKETING CAREER

ROBERT C HAWTHORN

61

If, despite your best efforts, the businesses that your competitors own always seem to come out on top of your own, then it might not be the dedication or work ethic or your team that is the problem, you may simply be basing your decisions on the wrong information. If you are afraid that this is happening to your business, then Data Analytics: An Introduction and Explanation into Predictive Analysis (How to Integrate Analytics into Your Business) is the book that you have been waiting for.

Inside you will find everything you need to know in order to start taking advantage of all the data that your business is already generating naturally. Over a quintillion bits of data are generated every single day and if you aren't thinking about how you can make the most of the parts of it that relate to your business, then your competition is likely already leaving you behind. So, what are you waiting for? Do your business a favor and buy this book today! It's what your competition doesn't want you to do.

Inside you will find
- A complete breakdown of the basics of data analytics and predictive analysis
- The secrets the pros use when it comes to data mining and data gathering
- The best beginner regression and machine learning techniques
- The best free programs to get you started
- *And more...*

62

Ready to tackle the forex world? Do you feel confident that you can join the largest financial market in the world and make a profit? It is okay if you say no, but you want to know more.

The forex market seems like a big mystery where you can make your cut of the $5 trillion traded in a day. It is, but you now have a book that is going to start helping you work through that mystery and learn what everyone trading in the forex market already knows.

You can make a quick profit, in a matter of minutes, with the right strategy. It all comes down to:

• Your comfort level with risk
• Your starting capital
• Your knowledge about the market

As you read through Forex for Beginners you are going to learn about

1. The history of forex
2. How forex works
3. How to start trading
4. Fundamental and technical trading analysis
5. Strategies to gain more profits

Start reading now, so you can be successfully trading in the forex market, with modest profits to start and better profits in the future. You have what it takes—now discover what forex traders know so you can pad your retirement account!

FOREX for BEGINNERS

A GUIDE TO DEVELOP YOUR FOREX
TRADING SKILLS AND KNOWLEDGE.

ROBERT C HAWTHORN

Are you looking to build new credit? Perhaps you wish to rebuild your credit? Maybe, you want better scores because you have heard how important they are?

Have you visited online websites and read the promises about increasing your credit scores in a matter of 30 days or even 90 days, only to find out that nothing you did worked?

Plenty of sites complete with testimonials perpetuate a magical, secret outlook when it comes to your credit scores, but are unable to deliver.

This book about credit repair is not offering you magic. It is offering you a dose of reality, with some personal experiences and true stories thrown in. The true stories are all personally verified. This type of information is better than articles on news websites or testimonials on random websites. However, these true stories are also less important to the overall meaning of the contents.

You are about to embark on a journey to build better credit and gain higher scores. You are asked to put effort and time into this journey towards a better financial appearance. It is the time and effort that will matter versus any magic secret someone else purports to have.

You will learn:
• The types of credit
• What the FICO score means
• Information about the credit bureaus
• 20 strategies for gaining better scores and a better credit history

If those four points are not enough, you are also going to discover:
1. Why you need time to build your scores
2. The key points to every strategy
3. How building on the first strategy with the next 19 strategies will help you in your goal

The one thing you are promised—you are not going to be given guarantees. You are not being told that you will gain 100 new points on your credit score. Instead, you will use those methods to clear up old information, build a better history, and in doing so raise your credit score for a better financial appearance on paper. When you go for a new credit, you will have a healthier creditworthiness that ensures competitive interest rates.

CREDIT REPAIR

BAD CREDIT

GOOD CREDIT

20 SUCCESSFUL STRATEGIES TO BUILD GREAT CREDIT AND INCREASE YOUR CREDIT SCORE.

ROBERT C HAWTHORN